First World War
and Army of Occupation
War Diary
France, Belgium and Germany

59 DIVISION
Divisional Troops
Royal Army Veterinary Corps
59 Mobile Veterinary Section
11 January 1916 - 28 February 1916

WO95/3019/1

The Naval & Military Press Ltd
www.nmarchive.com
Published in association with The National Archives

Published by

The Naval & Military Press Ltd

Unit 10 Ridgewood Industrial Park,

Uckfield, East Sussex,

TN22 5QE England

Tel: +44 (0) 1825 749494

www.naval-military-press.com

www.nmarchive.com

This diary has been reprinted in facsimile from the original. Any imperfections are inevitably reproduced and the quality may fall short of modern type and cartographic standards.

© Crown Copyright
Images reproduced by permission of The National Archives, London, England, 2015.

Contents

Document type	Place/Title	Date From	Date To
Heading	59th Division 59th Divl Mobile Veterinary Section 1916 Jan-1916 Feb And 1917 Jan-1919 Apl		
Heading	WO95/3019/1 59 Mobile Veterinary Section		
Heading	War Diary Of 2/1st North Midland Mobile Veterinary Section. From 1st January 1916 To 31st January 1916		
War Diary	St Albans	11/01/1916	26/01/1916
Heading	War Diary Of 2/1st N.M. Mobile Veterinary Section From Feb 1st/16 To Feb 29th/16		
War Diary	St. Albans	05/02/1916	28/02/1916

59TH DIVISION

59TH DIVL
MOBILE VETERINARY SECTION
~~FEB 1917-DEC 1918~~

~~APRIL 1919~~

1916 JAN — 1916 FEB
AND
1917 ~~JAN~~ — 1919 APL

WO95/3019/1
59 Mobile Veterinary Section

CONFIDENTIAL.

War Diary

of

2/1st North Midland Mobile Veterinary Section.

from 1st January 1916   to 31st January 1916.

(Volume 1)

Army Form C. 2118

WAR DIARY
or
INTELLIGENCE SUMMARY 2/1st N.M. Mobile Veterinary Section

(Erase heading not required.)

Place	Date	Hour	Summary of Events and Information	Remarks and references to Appendices
St Albans.	11/1/16	a.m.	Conveyed 18 horses from 2/1st Lincs Battery to No 2 Base Veterinary Hospital Luton	J.M.
"	12/1/16		Mobilisation equipment received in part.	J.M.
"	14/1/16	11 am	Inspection of Mobile Veterinary Section in Gorhambury Park by Col. DWYER. C.F.	J.M.
"	24/1/16	a.m.	Distributed 33 Remounts to 1/3rd Field Coy. R.E. Henley.	J.M.
"	26/1/16		Opened First Aid. Vet. Dressing Station in White Horse Stables. St Albans. 3 cases received	J.M.

CONFIDENTIAL

War Diary

of

2/1st N.M.Mobile Veterinary Section.

From. Feb 1st/16   To Feb 29th/16

(Volume 2.)

WAR DIARY or INTELLIGENCE SUMMARY

Army Form C. 2118

2/1 North Midland Division Mobile Veterinary Section

Feb. 1916   Page 1.

Place	Date	Hour	Summary of Events and Information	Remarks and references to Appendices
St. Albans	Feb 5th		One horse from 2/1 N. Mid. Field Ambulance, & one horse from 2/3 N. Mid. Brig. R.F.A. brought into Mobile Veterinary Section Dressing Station St Albans	G.G.S.
ST. ALBANS	9th		One horse from 2s & Co A.S.C. transferred to N. Mid Div. Vety. Hospital LUTON for treatment	G.G.S.
ST. ALBANS	10th		One horse from Headquarters Co. A.S.C. transferred to N. Mid Div.Vety Hospital LUTON for treatment	G.G.S.
ST. ALBANS	11th		One horse each from Staffs R.G.A. 2/3 N. Mid Bry. R.F.A., 2/4 N. Mid Howitzer Brig R.F.A. Transferred to N. Mid Div. Vety Hospital LUTON for treatment	G.G.S.
ST. ALBANS	12th		264. Pte Wells attached from N. Mid Div. Vety. Hospital LUTON, as batman	G.G.S.
ST. ALBANS	15th		Two horses from Moorq R.G.A. transferred to N. Mid Div. Vety Hospital LUTON for treatment	G.G.S.
ST. ALBANS	16th		One horse from 2/3 Field Ambulance transferred to N. Mid Div. Vety Hospital LUTON for treatment	G.G.S.
ST. ALBANS	7th		Horses of Mobile Vety Section inspected by COLSTOCK. D.A.D.R Vs 2 Circle	G.G.S.
ST. ALBANS	18th		One horse from 2/3 Bry R.F.A. transferred to N. Mid Div. Vety Hospital LUTON for treatment Nine horses transferred to Mobile Vety Section Dressing Station ST. ALBANS for treatment	G.G.S.
ST.ALBANS	25		One horse from 2/3 Field Ambulance transferred to Mobile Vety Section Dressing Station ST. ALBANS for treatment	G.G.S.
ST ALBANS	28		264. Pte WELLS returned to N. Mid Div Vety Hospital LUTON, owing to unfitness for overseas service	G.G.S.

Guy G. Scob
Capt A.V.C.

www.ingramcontent.com/pod-product-compliance
Lightning Source LLC
Chambersburg PA
CBHW081517160426
43193CB00014B/2711